<u>Raw Vegan Sauces and Salad Dressings</u>

Delicious and Nutritious Sauce and Salad Dressing Recipes

By: Kevin Kerr

In no way is it legal to reproduce, duplicate, or transmit any part of this document in either electronic means or in printed format. Recording of this publication is strictly prohibited and any storage of this document is not allowed unless with written permission from the publisher.

Table of Contents

Lemon Tahini Dressing (p.23)
Lemon Chia Dressing (p.23)
Basil Garlic Dressing (p.24)
Cherimoya Dressing (p.24)
Lemon Garlic Cashew Dressing (p.25)
Simply Spicy & Delicious (p.25)
Heaven on Earth (p.26)
Keep it Coming (p.26)
Anytime Blend (p.27)
Too Good (p.27)
Orange Pistachio Dressing (p.28)

Introduction

First off, all of these recipes would be impossible to make without a blender. All dressing recipes are suitable for 1 to 2 salads, up to 4 wraps, and sauces can be used for raw burgers, tacos, and burritos. Aside from tasting better, being better for your body, and being cruelty-free; uncooked vegan dressing and sauces take less prep time. I personally love these recipes and use one or more every day. Raw sauces are so beneficial for the human body because they practically digest themselves. Raw food is anything that isn't heated over 118 degrees so that the precious enzymes aren't destroyed. In order for food to digest it must be broken down by enzymes. Science has recently discovered that our bodies can only produce so many enzymes in this lifetime which is the number one reason to eat as much raw food as you enjoy. A great way to start is by trying the dressings and sauces!

Raw Hummus

- ½ cup sesame seeds
- 1 zucchini
- ½ cup tahini
- 2 tablespoons cold-pressed olive oil
- 1 to 2 tablespoons lemon juice
- 1 clove garlic
- ½ red bell pepper
- 1 or 2 red chillies
- sea salt to taste

Peel the zucchini. Put the sesame seeds in your blender and blend until nearly powdered. Add remaining ingredients and blend until smooth. Serves with raw vegetables, raw crackers, or use as a dressing for your salad or wrap!

Fresh Dill Dressing

- 2 tbsps. raw apple cider vinegar
- 1 tbsp. lemon juice
- 1 tbsp. diced red onion
- 2 tbsps. chopped fresh dill
- 1 avocado
- pinch of black pepper
- ½ tsp. turmeric
- sea salt to taste

Dressing of Love

- ½ cup soaked macadamia nuts
- ¼ cup pine nuts
- 2 pitted dried medjool dates
- 6 basil leaves
- 1 clove garlic
- ½ cup coconut water
- 1 tsp. hydrilla powder
- 1 tsp. marine phytoplankton powder
- 1 tsp. chlorella powder
- 1 tsp. spirulina powder
- sea salt to taste

Pink Panda

- 1 cup soaked sunflower seeds
- 1 cup cauliflower
- 1 chunk of beet root
- 1 tablespoon hemp seed oil
- 1 medium heirloom tomato
- 1 medium carrot
- squeeze of lime juice
- sea salt to taste

Good Green Finishing

- 5 grape leaves
- 1 cup broccoli
- ½ cup fresh chives
- 1 avocado
- 1 tbsp. olive oil
- ½ cup fresh cilantro or parsley
- 1 tsp. moringa powder
- 1 tsp. marine phytoplankton powder
- 1 tsp. hydrilla powder
- kala namak salt to taste

Satisfactory Sauce

- 1 nori sheet
- 1 avocado
- 1 tsp. sacha inchi oil
- 1 tsp. sesame seed oil
- 1 medium tomato
- handful of soaked almonds
- 1 broccoli stalk
- 1 tsp. bentonite clay
- 2 cloves garlic
- pink Himalayan salt to taste

Spicy Orange Sauce

- 1 avocado
- 1 medium cucumber
- 1 orange bell pepper
- 1 medium carrot
- 1 habanero pepper
- chunk of red onion
- sea salt to taste

Healing Sauce

- handful of soaked macadamia nuts
- 1 avocado
- 1 cup crimini mushrooms
- 1 clove garlic
- 1 cup broccoli
- 1 tsp. olive oil
- 1 small carrot
- 1 medium heirloom tomato
- small chunk of onion
- squeeze of fresh lemon juice
- sea salt to taste

Peppy Pepper Sauce

- 1 red bell pepper
- ½ small red onion
- ½ avocado
- 1 tbsp. hemp seed oil
- kala namak salt to taste

Creamy Celery Almond Dressing

- 3 stalks celery
- 1 cup soaked almonds
- 1 large heirloom tomato
- 3 cloves garlic
- 1 tbsp. olive oil
- pinch of sea salt

Skin Nourisher

- 1 large cucumber
- handful of soaked walnuts
- squeeze of fresh lemon
- 2 cloves garlic
- 2 tbsp. raw apple cider vinegar
- 1 tsp. hemp seed oil
- 1 tsp. bentonite clay
- 1 tsp. maca powder
- 2 probiotic capsules
- pink Himalayan salt to taste

Raw Mayonnaise

- 1 cup soaked raw cashews
- ¼ cup fresh cauliflower
- 1 to 2 dried pitted medjool dates
- squeeze of fresh lemon juice
- ¼ cup cold-pressed olive oil
- 1 tsp. raw apple cider vinegar
- ¼ cup water
- sea salt to taste

Raw Ketchup

- 1 ½ cups fresh diced heirloom tomatoes
- ½ cup sun dried tomatoes
- 1 to 2 dried pitted medjool dates
- ¼ cup cold-pressed olive oil
- 1 tbsp. raw apple cider vinegar
- sea salt to taste

Raw Mustard

- ⅓ cup water
- ¼ cup yellow mustard seeds
- ¼ cup brown mustard seeds
- ¾ cup raw apple cider vinegar
- 1 to 2 dried pitted medjool dates
- ½ tsp. turmeric
- sea salt to taste

For "honey" mustard add ½ cup maple syrup or more!

Raw Barbeque Sauce

- 1 cup soaked sun dried tomatoes
- 5 tbsp. raw apple cider vinegar
- ½ tsp. liquid smoke
- 1 clove garlic
- 2 tbsp. chopped red onion
- ¼ cup maple syrup
- 1 ¼ cup water
- juice of ½ lemon
- sea salt to taste

Raw Hot Sauce

- 4 oz. of your favorite hot peppers
- 1 cup raw apple cider vinegar
- 3 cloves garlic
- ½ tsp. chili powder
- 4 sprigs cilantro
- ¼ tsp. cumin
- juice of ½ lemon
- sea salt to taste

Raw Vegan Pesto

- 2 cups fresh basil
- ½ cup walnuts or macadamia nuts
- ½ cup olive oil or 1 avocado
- 3 tbsp. nutritional yeast
- 1 tbsp. fresh lemon juice
- sea salt to taste

Nacho Cheese

- ½ cup soaked sunflower seeds
- ½ orange red bell pepper
- 3 tbsp. nutritional yeast
- 2 tbsp. fresh lemon juice
- 5 tbsp. warm water
- sea salt to taste

Lime Avocado Dressing

- 1 avocado
- 2 tbsps. olive oil
- 2 tbsps. lime juice
- juice of 1 orange
- 1 green onion
- 1 small habanero pepper
- sea salt to taste

Mango Mustard

- 1 cup fresh mango
- 2 tsps. tahini
- 2 tbsps. raw mustard
- 1 tsp. raw apple cider vinegar
- 2 tbsps. water
- sea salt to taste

Italian Dressing

- ¼ cup olive oil
- ¼ cup chia or flax oil
- 6 tbsps. lemon juice
- ¼ cup raw apple cider vinegar
- ½ tsp. oregano
- ½ tsp. onion powder
- ½ tsp. dry basil
- 2 cloves garlic
- sea salt to taste

Thyme Sunflower Dressing

- ½ cup soaked sunflower seeds
- ¼ cup fresh thyme
- ½ tsp. dried basil
- ¼ cup water
- 2 tbsps. lemon juice
- 2 tbsps. olive oil
- ¼ tsp. kelp granules
- sea salt to taste

Raw Thousand Island

- 1 medium heirloom tomato
- ⅓ cup raw tahini
- 2 tbsps. raw apple cider vinegar
- pinch of cayenne pepper
- sea salt to taste

Mix in finely diced raw pickles after blending!

Spinach Walnut Sauce

- 3 cups spinach
- 1 clove garlic
- ½ cup walnuts
- ¼ cup water
- 1 tbsp. lemon juice
- 1 tbsp. olive oil
- ¼ tsp. nutmeg
- ¼ tsp. rosemary
- sea salt to taste

Creamy Pepper Dressing

- ½ cup cashew milk
- ⅓ cup raw apple cider vinegar
- 1 clove garlic
- 1 tsp. pink peppercorns
- 1 tsp. white peppercorns
- ½ tsp. onion powder
- 2 tsps. chia seeds
- sea salt to taste

Red Pepper Sauce
- 2 tbsps. pili nut butter
- 1 tbsp. lemon juice
- ¼ cup stone ground mustard
- 1 red bell pepper
- 1 clove garlic
- sea salt to taste

Raw Vegan Ranch Dressing
- 1 cup soaked cashews
- ¼ cup olive oil
- 3 tbsps. lemon juice
- ½ cup hemp seed milk
- 2 cloves garlic
- 1 tsp. dried dill
- 2 tbsps. fresh parsley
- ½ tsp. onion powder
- sea salt to taste

Almond Ginger Dressing

- ½ cup soaked almonds
- ½ cup almond milk
- 1 cup water
- 4 tbsps. raw tahini
- 6 pitted dried medjool dates
- 1 clove garlic
- 1 thumb-sized chunk of ginger
- sea salt to taste

Lemongrass Dressing

- 1 lemongrass core
- ¼ cup pumpkin seed butter
- 3 tbsps. raw apple cider vinegar
- 2 tsps. coconut sugar
- ⅓ cup water
- dash of cayenne pepper
- sea salt to taste

Lemon Tahini Dressing

- ½ cup raw tahini
- ⅓ cup lemon juice
- ¼ tsp. onion powder
- ¼ cup water
- sea salt to taste

Lemon Chia Dressing

- 1 lemon (peel and all if organic)
- 2 tsps. chia seeds
- 1 clove garlic
- ½ cup soaked cashews
- 1 cup water
- ½ tsp oregano
- 1 tbsp. fresh dill
- pinch of black pepper
- ½ tsp. turmeric
- sea salt to taste

Basil Garlic Dressing

- ½ cup olive oil
- 2 tbsps. raw apple cider vinegar
- juice of 1 lemon
- 2 clove garlic
- 10 basil leaves
- sea salt to taste

Cherimoya Dressing

- fruit of 1 cherimoya
- juice of 2 lemons
- 2 dried pitted medjool dates
- 1 clove garlic
- 1 tbsp. dried basil
- 1 tbsp. dried dill
- 1 tbsp. dried parsley

Lemon Garlic Cashew Dressing

- ⅔ cup soaked cashews
- 1 clove garlic
- ½ lemon (peel and all if organic)
- 1 tbsp. onion powder
- 2 tbsps. olive oil
- ¾ cup water
- sea salt to taste

Simply Spicy & Delicious

- 1 large or 2 medium heirloom tomatoes
- small chunk of red onion
- ½ serrano pepper
- 15-20 soaked almonds
- sea salt to taste

Heaven on Earth

- 20 to 30 fresh chives
- 1 medium heirloom tomato
- 1 avocado
- Squeeze of fresh lemon
- sea salt to taste

Keep it Coming

- ½ cup olive oil
- 1 tsp. of chlorella
- 1 tsp. of spirulina
- 1 avocado
- 1 tbsp. raw apple cider vinegar
- pink himalayan salt to taste

Anytime Blend
- 2 cups cherry tomatoes
- ⅓ cup of fresh basil
- 1 small red onion
- ¼ cup of raw organic apple cider vinegar
- sea salt to taste

Too Good
- 1/2 cup hemp seed oil
- 1 whole lemon (peel and all if organic)
- soaked sunflower seeds
- soaked pumpkin seeds
- sea salt to taste

Orange Pistachio Dressing

- 3 cups orange juice
- ¼ cup raw sesame seeds
- ¼ cup pistachios
- ¼ cup chives
- squeeze of lime juice
- 1 thumb-sized chunk of turmeric root
- sea salt to taste

89997270R00017